STARING INTO CREATIVITY

Ways To Be More Creative & Inspiration From Great Films And Literary Works

Written by
BLAKE BAZEL, M.S.

authorHOUSE®

AuthorHouse™
1663 Liberty Drive, Suite 200
Bloomington, IN 47403
www.authorhouse.com
Phone: 1-800-839-8640

First published by AuthorHouse 5/7/2009

ISBN: 978-1-4389-5269-7 (sc)

Library of Congress Control Number: 2009902848

Printed in the United States of America
Bloomington, Indiana

This book is printed on acid-free paper.

Front cover: *photo of painting by Blake Bazel*
Back cover: *publicity still photo of Marilyn Monroe*

photographs inside book
drawing by Marisol Blanco
publicity still photo of Gérard Philipe and Danielle Darrieux
publicity still photo of Erich von Stroheim
publicity still photo of Greta Garbo

Enjoy the beauty of nature— let it inspire the way in which you live

CONTENTS

Introduction

S TARING INTO CREATIVITY will encourage you to explore and discover the freedom that is essential to the creative Being. The path that we each take in life is unique. It is not where you start or how long it takes you to get somewhere that ultimately matters. All of our journeys of life will take us to different places at different times. Rather, it is important to always believe in yourself, and to appreciate the opportunity to exist in nature. This book will motivate you to be resilient and to continually strive for your goals.

In the first chapter, actress Julie Harris, composer Sándor Balassa, film director Milos Forman, Queen Sonja of Norway, and choreographer David Bintley discuss what is important to being a creative person. Then, in the following two chapters, selected themes from 20 films and 15 literary works are explored. Below each listed film or book is an important point(s) that is related to the story, and that can help guide you to have more creativity and happiness in your life.

Chapter Four profiles some of the most creative individuals in recent times, and includes a description of the qualities that enabled them to make great contributions to the Arts and Sciences. These are qualities that we can aspire to incorporate into our daily lives— to make some of their positive spirit come alive within ourselves, and enable us to make our lives more meaningful. The creative process begins with the visions, dreams, and goals that we have for ourselves— which comes about from the inspiration that we receive from others— the people who had the courage to express their individuality, and to pursue their endeavors and overcome obstacles along the way. Undoubtedly, these people had their flaws; since, imperfections are an inescapable part of life. But, we can appreciate their positive attributes and use them as a catalyst for exploring and utilizing the greatness within ourselves.

The Appendix contains letters from fascinating, creative personalities of the past. These manuscripts are intended to show the struggles and triumphs, and the perseverance and determination that are often characteristic of the most original thinkers. The letters reveal the spirit of the Artist — and, they are a reminder that you are not alone in your quest to experience a unique, meaningful life.

To my family and every person who yearns to express the creative Self and to live with sincerity, fulfillment, and hope.

CHAPTER ONE

What Do You Feel Is Important to Being a Creative Person?

The keys to being creative are to possess an active imagination, being open to suggestion, being willing to take healthy risks, listening carefully, staying up to date with current events, and reading everything you can get your hands on, even if it's something you don't think you'll like. Read poetry, take art classes, let your imagination fly. Stay away from video games and TV, and instead write your own stories, poems, and plays, even if you don't know how. Take classes during the summer, attend play-acting classes or puppetry, volunteer in any field, be active in the local library programs. In other words, open your mind to everything around you, ask questions about anything that strikes your fancy, don't accept stock answers but delve deeply. A "couch potato" will never be creative! Go for it!

Julie Harris, Broadway Actress

If you have any talent, you must use it for the other persons; family, friends, nation, mankind... Not important what kind of profession you work on, but your activity must be of the highest quality.

The real personal happiness you will get would be no other way!

Sándor Balassa, Hungarian composer

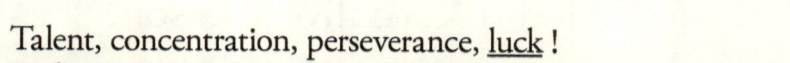

Talent, concentration, perseverance, luck !

Milos Forman, director of *A Fireman's Ball, One Flew Over the Cuckoo Nest*, and *Amadeus*

There are many reactions to contemporary art. Some are shocked. Others become enthusiastic. But, we are all, however, intrigued and we feel our curiosity tickled!

For a person like myself with a strong interest in contemporary art... meeting with new artistic expressions often provokes a change of attitude towards the unexpected and unknown.

Life is full of dreams and conflicts, poetry and drama. We find it all expressed- with beauty, sensitivity, despair and cruelty. The artists want each and every one of us to take part, in our own way... It is our right to have our own opinion. It is our own understanding, our own interpretation that counts.

H.M. (Queen) Sonja, Norway— personal sentiments on creativity and inspiration. Excerpt also appearing in speech from *Biennale of Venice 2003.*

"What do you feel is important to being a creative person?" is a very good [question] because it seems very simple, but is actually quite complicated!

When I was about five or six, I appeared on stage for the very first time. This wasn't on a professional stage, but part of the annual concert that took place at the church I used to attend when I was small. I suppose that was the very first time in my life that I realized what I wanted to do. I just wanted to be on stage, some people call it "stage struck."

When I was a bit older, ten or eleven, my sister used to go to a local dance class and I realized that this would be a good way of getting on to the stage more often, so I took up dancing. At the time I didn't do just ballet, but I also did tap, jazz and song and dance.

When I was thirteen, I saw my first ballet. From that point on I realized that I wanted to be in the world of ballet and a few years later, not really realizing what I was doing, I made my very first ballet. I didn't do this because I wanted to be a choreographer… because I didn't even know what a choreographer was at that stage! No, I made my first ballet in order that I might dance the leading role! However I enjoyed the experience so much that from that point onwards I realized that my ultimate aim was to be a maker of dance, a choreographer. I think this is because so much of what a choreographer does, working with music, working with scenery and costume designers and creating the steps for the dancers to do was of great interest to me and used all of my creative powers.

Ever since then, although other interests have come into my life, and other aspects of working in dance (I am also Director of a ballet company) I have never lost my love for choreographing. I suppose that this is at the heart of your question. All the experiences of my life feed my creativity and inspiration as a choreographer or "dance maker" and this has been my one true passion since I was a teenager. It's something I never tire of and I am very fortunate in that I can say my job is also my greatest interest and therefore it has never seemed like "work" to me.

Love what you do, and do it with passion!

David Bintley, Director of Birmingham Royal Ballet, London

Publicity still photo of Gerard Philipe and Danielle Darrieux

CHAPTER TWO

Ways to Be More Creative and Inspiration from 20 Great Films

I.   *Cléo from 5 to 7*, France, Agnès Varda, 1962

In the film, Cléo, a young singer, reflects more on her feelings and thoughts after she suspects that she has cancer. She becomes more sincere, independent, and confident.

Be Willing to Discover Who You Really Are

It is not an easy task to understand the self. Learning is a never ending process— whether it be about science, art, and/or yourself. There are times when you may feel that you can go no further and that the world will not allow you to progress. Instead of submitting to outside restrictions, use the disappointment to find a new path. Continually experiencing new opportunities is what allows for fulfillment and discoveries.

Find True Meaning in Your Life

One of the best ways to learn about the self is through your work. There could be times when the need to satisfy basic necessities influences you to pursue a certain job, and prevents you from devoting much of your time to the work that you desire. However, we are not limited to having one work identity. Artists and writers such as Rousseau and F. Scott Fitzgerald used one profession to support them financially while continuing to do the craft that they loved.

Break Away From People Who Restrict Your Personal Freedoms

You should not feel that you have to assume a certain identity when interacting with any person(s). You are not an image. You are a living, feeling and thinking individual. If you feel that certain people prevent you from spiritually and mentally growing, then be willing to break the bond.

Devote Some Daily Time to Solitude

Reflecting in solitude enables you to ask yourself questions, and respond with honest feelings and thoughts that are unaffected by the perceptions of others. Establishing the identity of the inner-self when alone makes you stronger, because you are not dependent on the presence of others for fulfillment. Also, it is a major source for ideas that will allow you to transcend beyond routines and banalities.

Love More Than You Fear

Appreciate each day that you are alive. Admire nature—the birds, the flowers, and people. Recognize the beauty of individuals and feel a freedom to extend friendship and love to others.

You cannot escape the hardships of life. But, you do have a choice— to be scared of an outcome or to make beauty from whatever you are dealt in life.

Find Your Greatness

Fulfill your dreams. Strive to be outstanding— not for others, but for yourself. At the end of your life, it would be nice to say, "I tried my best to live my dream."

The aim is not to meticulously follow a blueprint of life. This would be boring. Surprises, detours, and chance discoveries enable us to be creative and to achieve in a manner that we never expected.

II. *Doctor Zhivago*, U.S., Giacomo Campiotti, 2002
In the film, Zhivago makes many sacrifices to try to find more beauty and meaning in his world.

Have Ideals

Ideals are what let us ward off conformity. We develop our self-identity by acknowledging fantasies. Pursue the unforeseen, rather than settling for what already exists. If you can only achieve your ideal 1 out of 100 times, then it is that unique occasion that allows you to feel the ecstasy of life— a robust confidence in yourself and in your place in the world, and an exuberance to further define and discover truths of your existence.

Be Receptive to Your Emotions

It is important to allot time to experiencing and understanding your true emotions. Our feelings motivate us to go beyond ourselves and to pursue new directions in life. Emotions are a way of telling us to embark on new challenges (when we are happy), or to try novel approaches (when we feel disappointed or down).

Perfectionism is Restricting

Be spontaneous. Do not stop yourself because something is not going according to plan. We all feel uncomfortable when we are in a new environment or trying a new approach. Realize that positive change is not always easy or relaxing. Maintain some of the adventurous child in you. Make yourself vulnerable to some uncertainty and be willing to learn and change.

Persevere

Keep what is inherently important to you, and do not compromise your special qualities in times of adversity. You exist for an eternity if you live according to your true self, because your spirit resonates in the minds of others. Live to be authentic, and if you have misfortunes, then at least you never departed from your own terms of living. You may lose others and materialism, but you are never forced to lose yourself.

———————◆——◆———————

III. *Malena,* Italy-U.S., Giuseppe Tornatore, 2000
In the film, Malena is rejected by the townspeople because she is a very good looking woman. They reject the beauty that she has in her inner-self, because they view her as an object and not as a human being.

People Cannot Always be Judged by the Way They Look

Sometimes, we mistakenly believe that people will behave according to preconceived stereotypes, or in a similar manner to others who resembled them in our past. A beautiful woman who does not talk a lot is not necessarily unapproachable. She may be shy and alone, because people assume that she is above them— when in truth, she is kind and caring. Similarly, a man who is attractive and frequently smiles may be "happy-go-lucky" and not an individual with ulterior motives. Be aware that a person's looks <u>may</u> be deceiving.

Be Willing to Learn from the Experiences of Others

Be an observer. Appreciate the knowledge that you can take away from the successes and failures of others. Then, use this information to find your own unique approaches to everyday challenges.

When You Make a Mistake, Realize That Life Continues and That Your Actions in the Present Are Most Significant

Turn negative situations into positive moments. Don't think of how others will judge you from your mistakes. Instead, focus on making progress at the present moment. See the mistake as an inspirational source to find a new path in your life— a new approach that would have not come to fruition if it had not been for the error that had taken place.

When you experience a setback, resume work after a <u>brief</u> break. It is good to devote a limited amount of time to expressing and understanding your emotions that stem from the disappointment. Then, "get back on your feet" and move forward. Life is about learning from miscues and making adjustments that will make you a happier person.

Your reward for improving yourself from a mistake: self-pride, a building confidence, and favorable present circumstances overshadowing what occurred in the past.

IV. *To Catch a Thief,* U.S., Alfred Hitchcock, 1954

In this film, Cary Grant portrays a man who challenges himself to have new fulfilling experiences. Along the way, he experiences adversity, but the result of his efforts is that he has more meaning in his life.

Be Gutsy

Great accomplishments evolve from a person's audacity to be different. Work from your heart and try to make every moment of your life count. Continually challenge yourself by seeking new opportunities.

Be a Romantic

When people imagine what it is to be a Romantic, they may often visualize the lover who has the perfect word or kiss for an occasion. This is not the Romantic that is being discussed here. Instead, the Romanticism that I refer to is the individual who strives to attain his/her dreams and dares to be true to the self—even if at times it involves making the journey to success alone.

The Romantic seeks inner-adventures, aspires to continually learn, and has a great appreciation for nature. This individual understands that there is a purpose for existence, and that each day is a gift that allows for further exploration of the meaning of life.

V. *My Life to Live*, France, Jean-Luc Godard, 1962
In this film, Anna Karina portrays a woman who is self-reflective. She questions herself and the meaning of her existence. However, her downfall is that she has relinquished to others her freedom to follow her own path.

Don't Let Others Take Advantage of You

Trust yourself. When you feel that someone is not treating you properly, then confront him/her. Be confident in expressing your true thoughts and feelings to the other person.

Often, you may hear advisers say, "Play the game." It is this approach that causes disagreements and ruptures in relationships. Frequently, difficulties arise from misunderstandings. Thus, try to clarify issues in interpersonal relationships. In the best scenario, a beneficial relationship is reestablished. At worst, you are not misled into hoping for what cannot become an actuality. Then, you can test the person's integrity, and decide whether associating with him/her is worthwhile.

Being Loyal to Yourself

Temporary gain is not worth long-term humiliation. Avoid asking favors from people who do not share your values. Realize that it is better to live a true life, without ties to negative influences, than to be the quick beneficiary of fleeting perks. You always want to be in control of your core self— the integral attributes that comprise your identity. Once you lose this power, you live another person's life— being manipulated harshly to achieve their ends.

———————— ◆ ———— ◆ — ◆ ————————

VI. *Before Sunrise*, United States, Richard Linklater, 1995
In this film, Julie Delpy and Ethan Hawke portray persons who find fulfillment in a brief encounter.

Life is Brief— Be Daring and Create Opportunities for Yourself

It is better to try and fail to achieve your dreams, than to be content with an uninteresting, monotonous life. Maximize the opportunities that will allow you to go beyond yourself. Continually push yourself to seek new experiences. When there is an obstacle that delays your progress, then use that "break" to create greater opportunities. There is never a failure, as long as you continue searching for new paths and approaches to life during times of adversity.

Be Sincere to Yourself and Feel Free to Be Your True Self with Others

It is another person's loss if he/she does not accept your feelings and thoughts. Your "freedom to be who you are" is the foundation of your happiness. It is what will allow you to have a meaningful existence.

Make Time in Your Busy Schedule to Enjoy Yourself

Regularly devote time to pleasurable activities. People should not treat themselves as machines that are programmed to perform burdensome tasks. Otherwise, it will only be a matter of time before you, like the automated object, fall apart. When you devote time to yourself, you are reconnecting to the true purpose of life— which is the creation of positive moments that bring meaning into your existence.

Follow Your Aspirations

Your aspirations will not always come true. But, they can lead you in the right path, and present you with other attractive opportunities. Move forward, and with every new obstacle surpassed, you will feel an increase in confidence that will propel you further towards your goals.

Striving for your aspirations is what helps you to avoid "dead ends." They are your unique visions, and when challenges arise, they are important in helping you to find your own innovative solutions. Your goals are your blue-prints for life. Recognize that they can change— but, change does not mean settling for less.

VII. *The Red Shoes,* England, Powell & Pressburger, 1958
Moira Shearer portrays a woman who feels that Life is Art. She lives to dance. She experiences the passion, ecstasy, happiness, and challenges of existence.

Find Work or a Hobby That You Love

One of the main ways to experience a lot of meaning in your life is to discover an outlet that allows you to creatively express yourself. It is what motivates you to look forward to each day— even, if there are obstacles to be overcome. In part, we define our lives from the work that we have performed. Find an activity that you enjoy, and that will likely result in production that makes you proud.

Believe in Yourself

Most people do not start off at the top. Instead, they have to gradually work up to where they want to be in life. A dream does not mature into reality unless you have deep faith in yourself. Do not surround yourself with others who are not supportive. Stand up to people who do not treat you as a special person— by confidently making your presence known.

The world is full of possibilities. Thus, do not lose faith in yourself because of what happens at the moment. Accept the rises and falls of the present, but relentlessly focus on fulfilling your goals.

VIII. *A Man Escaped*, France, Robert Bresson, 1956

In this film, the lead actor portrays a man in a Nazi prison who is sentenced to death. While many others who are being detained in the prison have given up on life, this man finds a way to escape with merely a spoon, a few scraps from his room— and a desire to be alive!

Willpower Leads to Success

Success is not guaranteed. But, one thing is for sure. If you give up on something, whether it is a relationship, a career, or something else important to you, then you are not giving yourself a chance to succeed.

Life is about facing challenges. People who are persistent in their efforts will probably encounter more rewarding opportunities. Avoiding situations because of a reluctance to change will hamper your ability to be productive. Inevitably, there are times when you will have unfavorable and stressful experiences. Conceding defeat or settling for the status quo probably won't allow you to feel the joy of living. Instead, it is important to preserve the integrity of self, and to look for ways to make improvements for the future.

Learn from the Experiences of Others

The past is one of our great learning tools. Try to understand the success and mistakes of others. Then, implement these "lessons" into your approach towards life.

Norms Are Not Always Justified

Ultimately, you have to believe in yourself to make decisions about how to live. Sometimes you will be right, and other times you will be wrong. That is a given. But, it is your feelings and thoughts that matter most. If you take care of your own needs, then you will be in a better position to help others.

If you believe in a cause that is unpopular, then advocate it in your own way. You do not have to sacrifice your ideals because you are outnumbered. It is up to you to find your own meaning for existence. Sometimes that means being controversial or unpopular. Yet, it is your stance in support of "who you are" that increases your confidence and is empowering. The "I can win if I believe" feeling becomes a motivational force to success.

Keep On Moving Forward

There is not a "dead end" in your life, unless you look at the past as "would have" and "should have." We cannot change events that have already occurred, or erase bad memories. The past should be a learning tool, not a "reliving" tool.

We are all imperfect, and of course there will be times that we look back on more favorably than others. It does not pay to stress yourself over something that has already existed and that belongs to the past. When you worry about an event that has already taken place— that is on a "previous page of your life," then you take away the opportunities that you have in the present and future to improve your situation.

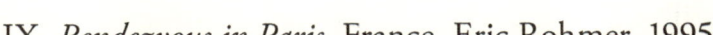

IX. *Rendezvous in Paris*, France, Eric Rohmer, 1995
In the first segment of this film, a college student confronts her boyfriend about his unfaithfulness. She reflects in solitude, and listens and confides to "positive" friends. She recognizes that moving forward in life means attempting to discover truth— whether it be pleasing or disconcerting.

It is Better to Know the Truth Than to Continue Deceiving Yourself

Make a change if you see or feel that something is not right.

Surround Yourself with Positive People or Just Grow in Solitude

Be very selective in choosing your friends. Give them opportunities to become positive influences by sharing some of your true feelings and thoughts.

Also, remember that it is better to have only yourself as your friend, than to be surrounded by people who are not supportive of your beliefs and endeavors. You can increase your knowledge and creativity in solitude; whereas, this becomes difficult when you are around people who you do not trust and who do not share your values. Then, relations become superficial— which leads to stagnation of the Self.

It Is Rewarding to Embrace Surprises in Your Life

Surprises can be the catalyst for progress and change. It gives us a flexibility to alter our path and approach in life. Monotony would be boring, and to try to live strictly by a plan can be stifling. The unexpected is a source for creativity, and it allows us to know that we are living— that we are a part of nature, where each day presents new opportunities.

Spontaneity is important for the experience of a meaningful existence. You remember the occasion when you found something that you least expected, more than the day that "goes according to plan."

X. *Torrent*, United States, Monta Bell, 1926

Greta Garbo portrays a woman who is heartbroken by the unfaithfulness of a man. While she enjoys acclaim as a singer, she does not allow herself to love again. She permits an unworthy man to cause her to avoid romance— and thus, she does not feel fulfilled. Materialism cannot replace love.

Be Willing to Love— Do Not Let a Bad Experience Deter You from Feeling Passion Towards Others

Be willing to love— it is inspiration for increased self-esteem, understanding of self, knowledge of the world, and creativity. There will be relationships with disappointing outcomes. However, that does not mean that every forthcoming interpersonal relationship will be marred by the same incidents that caused your pain.

If you give up on love, then you forfeit some of the greatest opportunities to have happiness in your life. You trade the chance of feeling ecstasy for avoiding pain. But, you are misleading yourself, because you cannot prevent pain from occurring. (You can limit the "bad pain" experiences— repeated mistakes. The "good pain" experiences— moving forward and continually learning from being creative and making mistakes— may initially hurt you. However, over time, "good pain" enables you to find more love, beauty, and knowledge in your life.) The denial of love leads you to experience more "bad pain," because you repeat the behavior of avoidance and fear – you are making the mistake of shunning love for a false security.

The experience of diverse emotions helps to define our lives. Our dreams, our hopes, and our goals are derived from our deepest feelings. Love is both pain and delight.

Don't Let Misfortune Build Up into Resentment

It does not do any good to hate another person for what he/she has done to you. Hate is a destructive emotion, and it causes you to be stuck in the past. Rather, feel pity for the person who is not worthy of your respect. Then, move forward with your life, and appreciate who you are as a person, knowing that there are better people to think about and spend your time with; thus, have an optimistic outlook. Don't let negative people of your past influence your view of the world— otherwise, you are being defeated and adversely changed by those people who do not deserve to be a part of your life.

The Benefits of Positively Expressing Emotions

Emotions encourage us to better ourselves from the past. Sadness and anger are an indication that we should search for new and different ways to improve the quality of our lives. Happiness and excitement inspire us to build upon our successes— to be willing to make positive changes while continuing along our life-path.

———————————◆·◆·◆———————————

XI. *Liebelei*, Germany, Max Ophüls, 1932

In this Max Ophüls film, two friends are very loyal to one another. One of the men made a mistake in his past, and he allows it to destroy himself and the life of the woman that he loves.

Recognizing and Understanding True Friendship

It is important to surround yourself with good quality people. However, it can be difficult to perceive whether a person is being sincere to you in his/her actions and words. Thus, you have to see through appearances and view the essence of the individual— to determine whether an authentic relationship exists.

Be true to the other person when you are trying to establish a friendship. Share some of your thoughts and values with the person. See if he/she shares important material with you. When this occurs, there is promise for a relationship of loyalty and trust— and, for a real channel of communication to exist.

Enjoy the friendship for each day it exists. But, if there are doubts that ever arise as to the state of the friendship, then re-analyze its reason for being. A relationship should not exclusively exist because of what happened in the past. The present is important too— warmth and kindness should be continually forthcoming.

The Past is Not an Excuse for Avoiding the Present

We have all made mistakes in the past. However, just because you have flaws, it does not mean that you cannot enjoy present opportunities. Mistakes are a path to new starts, not an end to enjoyment. Life is about falling and rising— and, there are always opportunities to rise, so long as you are willing to see them.

Misery is due to blindness towards the inner-self. It turns into suffering because the person refuses to see his/her world in any other way, except for the manner in which the mistake was made. Misery is tantamount to giving up and believing that your past is permanent. In reality, opportunities to make positive contributions to the self and world are abundant.

Your view of the world dictates the opportunities that are presented to you. If you are pessimistic, then you will convince yourself to "look the other way" when great opportunities are in front of you. When you have a positive outlook towards life, your mood and self-esteem are enhanced, and you are able to recognize many favorable circumstances that are continually entering your life.

XII. *The Legend of 1900*, U.S., Giuseppe Tornatore, 1999
In this film, a person who was born, abandoned, and raised on a cruise ship, becomes a piano prodigy.

Make the Most of Any Situation That You Are in– Do Not Feel Sorry for Yourself

Regardless of whether you feel your current predicament is good or bad, it is important to attempt to derive the most benefit from it for yourself. If the environment is restrictive, then explore your inner-resources. Maximize your individual creativity. Always try to produce and make something fruitful happen. Aspire to make a "negative" into a "positive" and an "ordinary" into the "extraordinary."

Creativity is Maximized When You Accept Adversity and View It as a Challenge

Focus on finding paths that will let you overcome challenges in your life. Adversity should not bee seen as a result. Instead, it should be viewed as a challenge that could inspire you to discover more meaning and creativity in your life.

XIII. *Le Bonheur*, France, Agnès Varda, 1965
In the beginning of this film, a husband and wife appreciate nature and its beauty in everyday life. They experience happiness by living life "their own way."

Having the Will to Live Differently Allows You to Be above the Superficialities of Everyday Life

Once you decide that you are going to live according to your own visions, you become liberated from feeling compelled to abide by trivial conventionalities of everyday life. Each step that you take towards a true, independent lifestyle emboldens you to live with more sincerity, and to have a greater determination to achieve your goals. Instead of sacrificing yourself for another's ideals, you focus on 1) better understanding yourself, and 2) perceiving the world as it relates to you. The result is an increase in self-esteem and feeling more content with your life.

Enjoy the Beauty of Nature— Let It Inspire the Way in Which You Live

When you get over-involved in the pressures of your daily life, reopen your eyes to nature. Feel the ocean breeze, or take a walk in the fresh air of the mountains, or admire the leaves of a garden plant— and savor these moments. Appreciate the wonders of nature, and the simple elements of life that can bring you happiness.

❖ ◆ ❖

XIV. *Cinema Paradiso*, Italy, Giuseppe Tornatore, 1989
In this film, a young man does not give up on life or in his admiration for a woman. He loves his work and overcomes obstacles.

Do Not Be Deterred by Rejection

When you believe in something, whether it is your work or your ideals, it becomes important to persevere in your quest for success. Another person's estimation of who you are, or of what you produce, is not the determining factor of your success.

People will have different opinions about you. We all have different feelings and thoughts. While you may encounter some people who are not receptive towards your efforts, there are likely to be others who will be positively affected by your contributions to society. It would be a shame to "give up" on your efforts to succeed in a particular area of life, because of an initial reaction from others. If you feel that what you are doing is good, then you should continue to convey your message. It is your duty to yourself, and undoubtedly, it will be help and inspiration to those who espouse your cause.

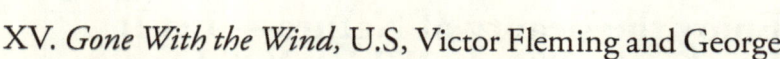

XV. *Gone With the Wind,* U.S, Victor Fleming and George Cukor, 1939

In this film, Scarlett is an admirably strong woman. However, her detriment is that she is not understanding of the feelings of Rhea and others in her family— until it is possibly too late.

Have a Balance Between Being Assertive and Being Sensitive

Sensitivity is what allows us to feel the meaningfulness of moments of our existence. It enables us to have understanding for others, to appreciate nature, and to be in touch with our true emotions. By understanding our sensitivities to the world, we can live and create with passion.

Also, it is important to be assertive. Make your own path, and be willing to follow your own initiative. Have the audacity to take favorable risks and to withstand adversity. Be novel, be resilient, and never let anyone lay claim to the core of your inner-self.

Be Selective

You deserve the best. Treat yourself as if you are Royalty. The truth is that you are King or Queen of your own world. Demand the most from yourself and from others.

XVI. *Ivan Rublev*, U.S.S.R., Andrei Tarkovsky, 1966

In this film, Ivan Rublev gives up hope for a period of time in being able to produce art for a deserving society. A young boy's actions inspire him to return to his art.

When You Believe in Yourself, Then You Exude Confidence to Others— You Become a Source of Inspiration — and, This Alone, is a Great Contribution to the World

There are many instances in which the difference between success and failure is the way in which you "carry yourself." Optimism encourages productivity. It energizes you to perform and to continue making improvements in the various aspects of your life.

When you feel success, it drives you on to further accomplishments. Then, your enthusiasm for life reverberates to other people. Your outlook towards a single person or event can motivate individuals that are unbeknownst to you— your inspiring approach to a situation(s) may positively impact many lives.

Continually Produce— Even If the Conditions or Situation Are Not Ideal

Our ideals are realized when we make movement towards them. Waiting for an "ideal opportunity" is a deceiving expression. You have to pursue what you desire. And, you will often incur inconveniences and flawed situations on your quests.

Regardless of the circumstances, try your best to actualize your aspirations. There are no perfect moments. Create opportunities for yourself, and innovate as a means to compensate for the imperfections that are in an environment.

XVII. *Sirens*, Australia/U.K., John Duigan, 1994

This film is based on the life of the Australian artist Norman Lindsay. He had a great appreciation for literature and expression of beliefs and feelings. He stood up for his convictions.

Learn from the Arts

The best teachers in the world are classic poetry and prose, and biographies of creative individuals. Seek to understand the spirit of both the artist and his/her creations.

Many artists had to struggle for a very long time in order to make their "breakthrough" in life. Use their experiences to better yourself. Use literature, music, plays, and film to identify unknown feelings and thoughts within yourself. Therefore, the Arts become a tool of self-discovery.

It is Fun to Be Unconventional

It is fun to just be yourself and to live for what matters most to you. Spontaneity is the exercise of freedom in your daily life. Have trust in yourself, accept your natural Self, and enjoy being a unique individual.

XVIII. *Bride of the Wind*, U.S., Bruce Beresford, 2001

In this film, the lives and times of Gustav and Alma Mahler, Klimt, Kokoschka, and Werfel are portrayed. Their love for art, and their great accomplishments and hardships are explored.

Find Beauty through Art

Transcend your daily experiences by finding a passion for the Arts. It is a way to freely communicate with yourself and the world.

XIX. *La Ronde*, France, Max Ophüls, 1950

In this film, it is shown how our experiences in life are fleeting. We are not defined by one moment. We can continue to make self-discoveries and have new experiences.

Life is a Merry-go-Round— If You Miss Out on an Opportunity, Just Make Sure to "Jump Aboard" When It Comes Around Again

We usually have many opportunities in life. Inevitably, we are going to miss out on some experiences. Therefore, do not be overly dismayed if an event and/or if a moment to take action evades you. It may not come around another time in its exact, previous form. But, you will likely have the opportunity to seize it again in near approximation to what is was— and, it may even be better than what you had previously believed that you "lost out on."

Life is about Love

There are two forces that are continually playing against one another— love and envy. Envy causes one to feel as if life is solely a competition— that others can never be trusted, and that if you do not defeat another, then you will be the one who is defeated.

When you allow yourself to love humanity, you become better able to work through misunderstandings, find solutions to problems, enjoy time with a variety of people, and discover new opportunities that are presented to you by others. You become less afraid of losing a part of who you are to another person, and instead, look forward to being able to share and learn with people who show that they are supportive of you. You don't lose faith because some people have treated you badly. There is the understanding that you have to move on when there is a disappointment. And, even if you encounter more disappointments than pleasurable experiences, it is the one new friend, or one new opportunity that makes your willingness to extend your kindness to others worthwhile.

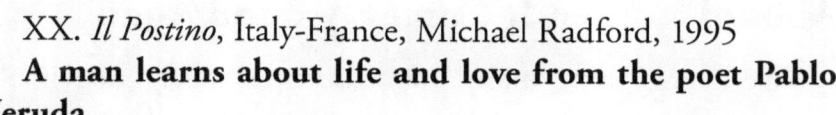

XX. *Il Postino*, Italy-France, Michael Radford, 1995
A man learns about life and love from the poet Pablo Neruda.

Knowledge from Nature

Increased creativity and self-knowledge often occurs after time is devoted to observing nature. The sea, mountains, and stars in the sky can enable you to feel reinvigorated and inspired to produce something that is original and meaningful.

CHAPTER THREE
Ways to Be More Creative and Inspiration from 15 Great Literary Works

I. *Lélia*, George Sand, 1833

This was George Sand's most self-revealing novel. It shocked Victorian-era society by advocating equality for men and women. Lélia is a sensitive and compassionate artist, but she has difficulty satisfying her longings for love.

Be Passionate about Life and Its Possibilities

Life is not only about work. Life is not only about a relationship. If one thing is not going well for you, then don't let it negatively affect your entire outlook on the world.

Often, we may get "carried away" by one event in our life. However, it is good to remember that there are many great opportunities that are awaiting us.

II. *The Last Summer*, Boris Pasternak, 1934

This novella takes place in 1916 when a young Russian man reminisces about the months before World War I. The novella explores his feelings and observations of nature.

The Inner Self

You may remember fun times in your childhood, when you played with your building blocks or dolls, and enjoyed being in an imaginary world. You would create plots and for hours you would be absorbed into unfolding dramas. We may disregard some of our toys as we get older, but it is still important to have a dream world. It is a way to reduce some of the stresses from daily life, and it can be a source of inspiration and creativity.

Also, fantasies can allow us to cope with difficult situations. Your imagination can provide happiness in times of outer-world sorrow. It is not an escape from "real life," but rather the experiencing of an "inner life"—in which we can go beyond the limits of time and space of our normal day, and find solutions and possibilities that will enhance our overall quality of life.

III. *Bruges-la-Morte*, Georges Rodenbach, 1892

A man deals with the death of his wife by fantasizing that her spirit is in another woman.

The Image of a Person That You See May Not Be the Truth

There may be times when we want to see a person in a certain way. But, remember— no one can take the exact role of another person in our life.

Be open-minded in your assessment of all people that you meet. Treat them as unique individuals. Your expectations for how they should act may not correspond with their truth of living. Each person is a mystery. Look forward to being surprised by another person's unique approach to life and/or talents. Renew your understanding of an individual on a daily basis. A person is not an image— and, if treated as one, then it is likely you who will feel hurt and deceived.

Appreciate the Unknown of the Future— It Is a Key to Creativity

You may have ideas about what will occur in the future, and that is fine because it allows you to make investments that will potentially benefit yourself. However, worrying about the future wastes your time today, has no effect on what will happen tomorrow, and forces you to limit the possibilities that await you.

Creativity is about giving yourself a freedom to explore life. The future is uncharted territory that has an abundance of resources that can be used to increase spiritual wealth. Have a tentative blueprint of what you may want to do—then, improvise and make adjustments in response to the changes in your life.

IV. *Maldoror*, Comte de Lautréamont, 1869

This literary work shocked many when it was first published because of its dark imagery. However, to the Surrealists and many artists, it represents the spirit of rebellion and the courage to be different.

Find New Ways to Your Success— Be Novel

People often feel that something new, regardless of how great it may be, is taboo. In both art and science, the innovators were frequently criticized and sometimes punished for their foresight.

Use this precedent to give you the resiliency that is needed to create.

The world is improved by people who are willing to be original, and depart from what is customary. Most people have the capacity to create. But, they often do not have the attitude that is a prerequisite for ingenuity. Have pride in finding alternative approaches to life. Look beyond initial reactions to your thoughts, and put your faith in their potential to enable progress to take place in the world.

V. *The Little Prince*, Antoine de Saint-Exupéry, 1943

A man crashes his plane in the desert and meets "the little prince" who helps him find more meaning in his life.

Make Each Activity of Your Life a Special Occasion and Look for Meaning in Everything— Even in Activities that Most Others Would Consider as Trivial

It is important to appreciate the gift of life that we possess— whether it be discovering the unexpected, seeing a beautiful person, or reading an interesting story. Everything that you see or feel is unique. You may interact with an insensitive person, and have your work shunned by a group of people. But, examine your environment closely at all times, and find something that is representative of the beauty of life. There is always something special to notice in every situation, because there are always the marvelous wonders that lay within yourself.

VI. *Faust*, Johann Wolfgang von Goethe, 1808

Faust is frustrated by the monotonous pursuits of society. He does not want to conform, and he pursues a life of adventure, passion, and purpose.

Continually Push Yourself to Go Further on Your Quest for Discovery

In order to sit up straight, you have to push yourself to not give into gravity. Similarly, you have to push yourself to have daily experiences beyond the ordinary. Be willing to put yourself in new situations, even if you feel uncomfortable because of the novelty of the environment. Change will often be accompanied by a nervousness or uneasiness. When we are young, we often get a "push" by parents, teachers, or friends to go to school on the first day, to ask a "crush" out on a date, and to seek a job. But, as we get older, the responsibility of encouraging us to move forward is placed upon ourselves. Once this is realized, you can take the action necessary to make your life more interesting: to seek new challenges, to feel the excitement that surrounds taking a potentially positive risk, and to know that while it may take effort and feel unnatural to act in a novel way, the benefits of success will make your endeavor worthwhile.

Be Willing to Explore Your Own Path

The only person who truly knows what you need and desire is yourself.

Continue to Learn

Try to discover new thoughts and feelings that will increase the meaning that you derive from life. Look forward to new opportunities, and challenge your own and others' pre-established ideas. The pursuit of knowledge and understanding will enable you to feel more vigor and renewal of the Self—

where every day becomes a new chapter of life that is full of insight and hope.

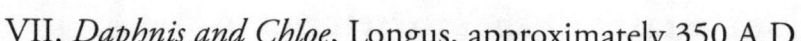

VII. *Daphnis and Chloe*, Longus, approximately 350 A.D.
Two young lovers are separated, and they overcome many obstacles in order to be reunited.

Focus on Being Productive in the "Here and Now"

We all have to deal with misfortunes in life— some people have had worse experiences than others. Be resilient and be strong. Difficulties from the past do not have to be your defining point. Find a path that lets you alter your course in life.

Do not try to judge the worth of yourself, because it only matters that from hereon out, you value your attributes with the highest regard possible. The respect that you have for yourself is what will let you get beyond the obstacles of life. Other people may have contributed to your misfortunes. But, it is You who always maintains control of your will, determination, and perseverance.

XIII. *Tess of the D'Urbervilles*, Thomas Hardy, 1891
The inner-beauty of Tess is rejected by her family and the outside world. She is a strong woman and perseveres through extreme misfortunes, only to be ultimately punished by a rigid and callous society at the end of the book. Her individuality, virtuosity, and passion for nature make her distinctive from the other characters in the story.

Beauty is Derived from the Spirit in Which You Live

People often focus their attentions on the results that are produced— such as winning, making, money, getting a high grade, or having an impressive job title. However, beauty is defined by the ways in which you approach living.

Falling short of a goal does not equate to failure or rejection. Otherwise, each person's life, even those who you most admire, would be inundated with misfortune. Defeat is when you do not achieve a result, and in the process of which you have sacrificed your identity in order to please others and not the Self.

Regardless of any result, focus on making your inner-self stronger. Do not sacrifice the keys to your Being. Then, you have impacted the world in a special and unique way—you have shared the truth of your Self.

* ◆ ◆ ◆ *

IX. *Of Lena Geyer*, Marcia Davenport, 1936
This novel follows the life of Lena Geyer— her struggles and triumphs in becoming a great opera soprano.

Independence and a Power of Self Come from Immersion into Art

Spontaneity, freedom, experiencing of varying emotions, and the power to create your own world are promoted in the Arts. All of these components contribute to a high self-esteem. Just as there are no exact rules to art, there are no laws in life that pronounce how you have to be and what path in life that you have to follow.

Being involved in the Arts allows you to feel the power of going beyond the commonplace. It helps you to understand your real thoughts and feelings pertaining to life. You can be the artist and/or the spectator of an art. Either way, you identify meaning and truth for the Self from the creative expression that is taking place.

Devotion to Your Creative Outlet Increases the Purpose and Meaning in Your Life

Naturally, your ideas will be incorporated into what you do— and, your energy will survive through your creative product. You feel an increase in purpose when you know that your effort resulted in creative output.

◆

X. *A Very Long Engagement*, Sébastien Japrisot, 1994
The widow of a World War One soldier embarks on a discovery to find out the circumstances of her husband's death.

In Times of Difficulty, We May Experience a Most Profound Kindness from Certain Others, and Realize New Approaches to Life

We all will experience difficulties. We may feel letdown, hurt, and uncertainty in our lives. However, it is often during these stressful times, that we are able to notice who is truly sincere and genuine around us— those who will be empathic and understanding of our condition. Whether it is a pat on the shoulder, a hug, or a speech of encouragement, it becomes possible to see that there are caring and nurturing people who want the best for us. And, if you do not see these people in your life, it is a signal that you have to open up to others, and give them the opportunity to be there for you— that you have to replace the negative people in your life with positive influences.

It is difficult times that let us know that we have to make positive changes in our lives. Emotional pain is a warning to the mind that approaches to life have to be changed. This sense perception is intended to be a temporary alert, not an agent of long term suffering and unhappiness. Emotional pain is a signal that tells us to "not give up"— to keep on searching for solutions to better our lives. Therefore, do not lose hope on your Self or on Life.

Pursue your goals with a conviction that you are going to keep on this mission— that you are going to persevere.

Stories Can Be Told in Different Ways. Look for the Positive Story and Don't Overemphasize the Negative Perspective. Anything can Be Criticized If That Is One's Intentions

It is important to notice problems and weaknesses. However, it is not worthwhile to linger over imperfections and mistakes, at the expense of being able to realize the benefits of an action/outcome.

Try to be open-minded and to perceive situations from differing perspectives. Then, attempt to make decisions and changes that are reflective of all of these observations.

———————— ◆ ◆ ◆ ————————

XI. *The Blue Flower*, Penelope Fitzgerald, 1995
A fictional story based on the life of Novalis— the suffering and triumphs that he experiences in romance and art.

The Benefit of the Art of Solitude— Talking to Yourself, Writing to Yourself— Communicating with Yourself

We talk to people to try to tell them who we are and what we feel. Since we would like others to try to understand ourselves, it should follow that we would want to continually know more about our "Being." The study of self requires solitude— a time when you are willingly by yourself to fulfill needs of privacy, meditation, and goal-setting.

Solitude involves thinking. It is the examination of what we enjoy in our lives, as well as the realization of what hurts us in life— and how to overcome the pain and better ourselves. In solitude there is a talking to the Self— a dialogue between the "I" who exists in the outside world, and the "I" who is your true spirit.

The coming together of these two *"I"s* helps you to feel authentic and complete. It reaffirms belief in yourself, because you better understand the core of yourself— your values and your inner-thoughts. They are not being disregarded and you are supporting them by recognizing their existence, and considering them in the formulation of future plans. This enhances your confidence and your self-esteem; because, you are not avoiding the inner-self "I" in order to please others with superficialities.

Creativity Comes from People Who at Times Approach Life by Going "Outside the Lines"

"Big things" can only happen when you dream **big**. Have a practical plan that can accommodate your needs. But, do not limit yourself by saying that "this cannot be done because it is not likely to happen." The greatest inventions and the most awe-inspiring performances were achieved because people believed in their fantasies and their dreams. They were willing to be different.

XII. *The Virgin and the Gypsy*, D.H. Lawrence, 1930

A young woman's life changes and she is liberated from past, restricting conventionalities. She embraces the freedom to find love and her own meaning in life.

You Are Not Alone in Your Pursuit of Finding a New World of Meaning. Past Creative Individuals Have Found Ways to Escape Suppression So That They Could Satisfy Their Dreams

Many creative people have overcome adversity such as abuse, poverty, and disabilities in order to find a life with more meaning. If you get "down" on yourself, because you feel that you always have to work hard just to make a little gain in life, or because it is taking too long to make progress, then explore the lives of people in both literature and biographies. See how they struggled and how they fought to persevere. Use their spirit to spur you on in your goals.

◆ ◆ ◆

XIII. *The Crying of Lot 49*, Thomas Pynchon, 1965

A woman finds out that she is the executrix of an estate. In the process of dealing with the chaos of the impending situation, she makes self-discoveries and finds new paths in her life.

Accept Some Chaos and Disorder in Your Life

There is not an answer or a reason to everything in life. We live in a chaotic world with many contradictions. It is the "unpredictable" and incongruities of life that allows an individual's imagination to freely come up with unique ideas and thoughts. Beauty does not always appear in front of our eyes. It may have to be sorted out and identified from within the entanglement of superficialities and disruptions that are magnified in the world.

XIV. *The Fountainhead*, Ayn Rand, 1943

Ayn Rand's story depicting the life of an architect named Howard Roark. Roark has to overcome many injustices along his path to becoming an innovative architect. He always believes in himself, and he never sacrifices his Self for another person. Ultimately, he succeeds in his mission.

View Difficulties as Only a Temporary Delay in Your Journey to Success

Do not be discouraged by the struggles and disappointments that occur in life. View these times as "challenges" on the way to achieving your goals. If you want to do something special, then you have to be willing to stay positive and work through the times that are not pleasant.

Goals and plans are not achieved easily. Finding success for yourself is not about walking into glory. It is about being focused on what you want to achieve when things do not seem to be going your way. Most of all, believe in yourself, and know that no matter what the result turns out to be, that you are a success if you tried your best and never gave up in your pursuit of something that would mean a lot to you.

XV. *Le Calvaire*, Octave Mirbeau, 1887

The narrator of the story initially has success as a writer. However, he sacrifices "who he is" for a woman and stops authoring stories. He becomes dependent on others and

suffers because he no longer knows his identity as a human being.

Continually Produce Novel Ideas and New Work

Give yourself the opportunity to find your own greatness. Be productive and be innovative. Do not allow yourself to "come to a stop" because of distractions or pessimism.

Nobody can stop you from being creative. <u>No person(s) can take away your desire and your capacity to find a way to produce something that is meaningful to the Self.</u>

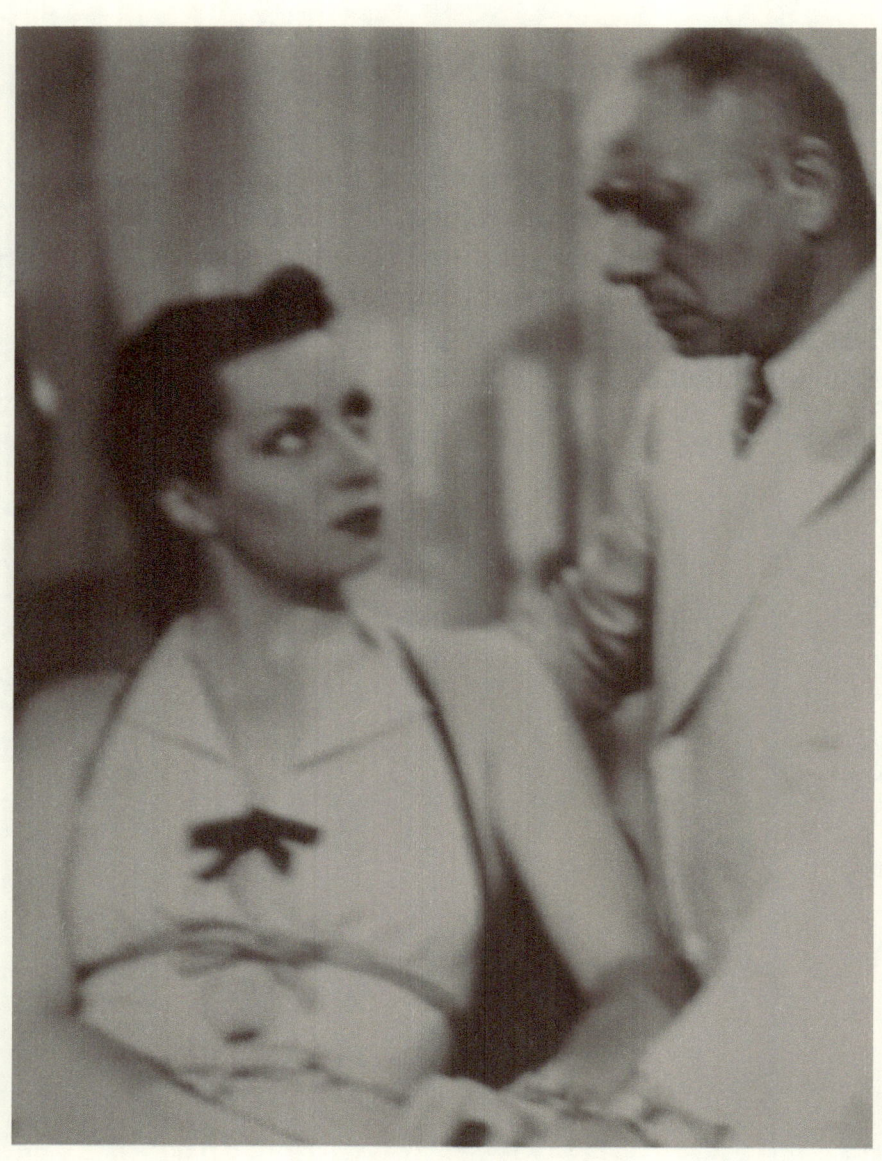

Publicity still photo of Erich von Stroheim with an actress

A Peak into the Lives and Admirable Qualities of Some of the Most Creative Individuals in Recent Times

BE WILLING TO FURTHER EXPLORE THE LIVES OF THESE PEOPLE. WE CAN LEARN A LOT FROM EXTRAORDINARY INDIVIDUALS OF THE PAST— BY BECOMING FAMILIAR WITH THEIR INSPIRATION, THEIR IDEAS, AND THEIR APPROACHES TO LIFE.

Isadora Duncan, dancer (1877-1927)

Isadora Duncan did not allow her impoverished childhood to prevent her from finding her greatness. She developed her own, unique dance style. She did what she felt was "right" in her heart, even when it meant receiving severe criticism. Isadora Duncan broke conventions— she gave birth to two children out of wedlock. She expressed her views to the outside world, even though they were not always consistent with the mainstream. Most importantly, Isadora Duncan did not give up on life when her two children tragically drowned, through the break-ups in her relationships, or from the adversity that she faced as a result of her honesty.

Grace Kelly, film actress, princess (1929-1982)

Grace Kelly was not the favored child in her family. However, she believed in her dreams, and she took on challenges in which she was not expected to succeed. While her parents believed that she would not be successful pursuing a modeling and acting career in New York, Grace Kelly not only persevered, but she became a great success. She worked hard to make herself a better actress, and she did not settle for less in her life. After her acting career, Grace Kelly became Princess of Monaco and a great patron of the Arts.

Erich von Stroheim, film director and actor (1885-1957)

Erich Von Stroheim was an idealist. Before he started his career, he changed his name to signify that he was descended from European royalty. In his early career, he was an assistant to the pioneer film director, D.W. Griffith. It was not long before Von Stroheim was directing his own films.

He was meticulous about portraying every detail according to his vision of the project— even specifying what type of underwear should be worn. Erich Von Stroheim's films were long and have often been considered as early cinema masterpieces. Von Stroheim would often get embroiled in arguments with producers, because of his insistence that his films not be compromised. He believed in his own creative talent and stood up to others who intended to alter his creative work. Von Stroheim's creative spirit and films have had an influence on many people involved in the Modern Arts.

Helmut Newton, photographer (1920-2004)

Helmut Newton was a photographer of fashion models and celebrities. He preferred to take nude pictures of women. He approached photography as an art— getting the woman to make the pose that he desired, and to give the face that would help set the theme of the photo shoot.

Helmut Newton was adamant about having his own style. He did not want to pretend to be something that he was not— Newton had no pretensions about being a cultural aesthete. His world revolved around the female nude who was all-powerful. It was his unique visions that enthused women worldwide to be a model for him. He continually challenged himself through his work, and he found "positives" from the difficult times in his life.

Amadeo Modigliani, painter, sculptor (1884-1920)

Amadeo Modigliani followed his dream. At an early age, he was not expected to survive pleurisy. After being diagnosed with this ailment, he was determined to be an artist.

Initially, his novel approach to painting was not embraced by many art dealers. People could not understand the reason for the elongated bodies that appeared on his sketches and canvasses. But, this did not prevent Modigliani from finding his own way as an artist. He refused to compromise his values for others, even when it meant that he would have to continue to live without financial and emotional support for his art.

Modigliani had a great appreciation for poetry and the Arts. He used these resources to inspire himself during the gloomy times of World War I, and when there were many detractors who refused to notice his merit. Modigliani could have abandoned art because of his lack of receptive audience. But, his work was meaningful to him. He was confident in the message that he had for the world— to show the inner truth of people and to go beyond the superficialities of life.

◆

Suzanne Valadon, painter (1865-1938)

Suzanne Valadon never received formal artistic training. She used her innate talent, and taught herself from the masters that were present in her environment. Valadon lived freely, and she was willing to defy social conventions that would be inhibiting to her in life. She experimented with different lifestyles, until settling on one that best befitted her ideals. Valadon was generous with fellow artists and exuberant about sharing her ideas and experiences with them. Suzanne Valadon became one of the great Modern artists of her time, because she believed that there were no barriers that could prevent her from following her dreams.

◆

Egön Schiele, painter (1890-1918)

Egön Schiele always dreamed of being an artist as a young child. His father preferred that he assume another profession. But, Schiele knew what he wanted to be, and what he had to be in life. Teachers at his art school tried to prevent him from expressing himself in the manner that he preferred. Schiele was not deterred in his efforts to develop a new approach to painting. He formed his own group and eventually left the school when he believed that they were holding him back in his career.

Schiele painted controversial portraits of women, and he was arrested and unfairly treated by the police in the Austrian village of Neulengbach. During his short imprisonment, he painted modern watercolor masterpieces— which were to be some of his best works. When he was released, Schiele continued to paint and to innovate until his untimely death.

Schiele had confidence in himself. His goal was not to win the acceptance of others. Egön Schiele wanted the right to produce his own art in his own way, and he realized that success is about not surrendering your beliefs when there is adversity.

Anaïs Nin, writer (1903-1977)

Anaïs Nin was a sensitive and kind woman, a talented writer, and a supporter of fellow artists. She lost contact with her father at an early age, and she had lived in many countries before she was a teenager. Despite the lack of stability in her early life, Anaïs Nin was determined to find herself as both a person and an artist. She began her career as a dancer. Nin was introspective and she used Analysis to help her to explore her strengths and weaknesses. By making positive changes throughout her life, she continued to increase her self-esteem.

When Anaïs Nin could not find a publisher that was receptive to her writings, she decided that she would manually print her own books. Soon, they became very successful, and publishers were vying to hold rights to her works. Nin opened up to the artistic community and to the world— sharing her experiences and thoughts with her readers. In turn, they provided her with more material for her writings.

Anaïs Nin devoted a lot of time towards making a happy existence for herself. By attending to her own needs and desires, she was able to have great creative output. And since she was satisfied with who she was as a person, she was prepared to genuinely help others to find meaning in their lives.

Ingrid Bergman, film & stage actress (1915-1982)

Ingrid Bergman pursued her interests as a child— photography and acting. She had great success as an actress in Sweden. When she came to the United States, she was determined not to sacrifice her inner-self or change her appearance in order to please Hollywood film executives. Throughout her career, she demanded powerful roles, and embraced challenges that would allow her to develop further as an actress.

In the late 1940s, a married Ingrid Bergman fell in love with Roberto Rossellini, the famed Italian film director. She would not compromise her passion for the sake of satisfying the American public. Ingrid Bergman understood that it is most important to be loyal to yourself, and that the public is fickle. She continued to have great success as an actress. While other female film stars disappeared from movies and the stage as they grew older, Ingrid Bergman remained prominent because of her perseverance, determination, and motivation to fulfill the expectations that she had for herself.

T.S. Eliot, poet, playwright (1888-1965)

T.S. Eliot was a man full of contradictions: proper in public, but rebelling in private; sensitive and concerned about the outside world, yet, inclined to avoid persons and situations in his life. Through his writing, he expressed the true voice of a real human being, plagued by the chaos and difficulties presented by a Modern world.

The beauty of Eliot's creativity comes from his honesty— his perception of the world that he shares with his readers. Whether it be his evaluation of the world or of himself, it is possible to understand the true Eliot. His message is unique— there are many obstacles in the world, but that the path to meaning is by being a true, feeling and thinking human being.

T.S. Eliot experienced adversity throughout his life. He used these challenges to increase his creative output, to define who he was as a person, and eventually to find happiness in an intimate relationship.

Marilyn Monroe, film actress, model (1926-1962)

Marilyn Monroe was in an orphanage for much of her early life. In her youth, she was continually changing schools, and she was not always accepted by her peers. However, these early hardships did not deter Monroe from aspiring to satisfy her dreams. Marilyn Monroe overcame obstacles and became one of the most accomplished actresses and models of the 20th century. Also, through self-learning, she became a part of the intellectual vanguard— reading modern classics that were penned by the likes of Carl Sandburg and James Joyce. She developed friendships with some of the greatest thinkers of the era.

Marilyn Monroe evolved and changed throughout her life. She refined her drama skills at the Actor's Studio, and she eventually performed serious film roles. Monroe was a very introspective person, who devoted time to trying to understand her true feelings. She had flaws, but she was not the starlet who was lost in the world. Instead, Marilyn Monroe was an individual who was intent on improving herself and the lives of others.

Robert Desnos, poet, writer (1900-1945)

Robert Desnos became recognized in the 1920s as one of great Surrealist poets. His automatic writing achievements won him great acclaim throughout Western Europe. Desnos was adamant about following his own life plan. It would have been easy for him to settle for a comfortable life after his early success. But, he split with the leader of the Surrealists, André Breton, because he wanted to continue to express himself through his own writing style.

Desnos was committed to developing his creativity. He would take risks throughout his writing career. But, he would never sacrifice the values that meant most to him. When the Nazis invaded France, Desnos became very involved in the Resistance. Eventually, he was denounced and transported to concentration camps throughout Europe. He died shortly after his concentration camp was liberated by the Allies. Then, the heroics of Densos during these times became known to the world— how he would share his resources with others who were suffering, and how he would defy and stand up to the Nazi officers. In times of good and bad, Robert Desnos continued to have confidence in himself and his unique vision. He never gave up hope, even in the midst of some of the darkest days that this world has ever seen.

Gérard Philipe, film actor (1922-1959)

Gérard Philipe's life was cut short at the zenith of his career—as he heartbreakingly died from cancer. But, from an early age to his last day alive, Philipe was always looking forward, trying to find more meaning and fulfillment in life. At a young age, Gérard Philipe took risks that would enable him to attain his ideals. Philipe auditioned for parts in plays, and gradually garnered the admiration of directors and fellow actors. He had leading roles in theatre and film productions in the 1950s.

Gérard Philipe's warmth towards humanity and his work for social causes positively impacted the lives of many people who were just overcoming the hardships of war. Philipe was willing to be controversial, in order to be sincere to his inner-self and to the world. He wanted to be more than an enchanting silver screen face. Gérard Philipe desired to have a life full of purpose and beauty.

Jacob Epstein, sculptor (1880-1959)

Jacob Epstein was insistent on becoming a sculptor from an early age. His family did not support his artistic dreams. Nevertheless, Epstein was determined to make monumental sculptures that would convey his personal message to the world.

Initially, he struggled in his efforts to launch his career. Epstein emigrated from New York to London. Then, his work began to attract the attention of critics and the public. Some people believed that his sculptures were profane. Others believed that they were not worthy of being placed in public spaces or in museums.

Jacob Epstein had to overcome anti-Semitism and an intolerance of his fierce individuality. He was very confident in who he was as a person and in the great possibilities that were awaiting him in the future. Epstein was enthusiastic about being unconventional and about provoking change in the way that people viewed the world. He was ready to stand up to any person or institution that acted inappropriately towards him.

Jacob Epstein was a visionary and a strong person who refused to submit to people who tried to use their status to impose upon his life. By having a firm conviction in his self-worth, Epstein became one of the most admired artists of the 20th century.

◆

Hedy Lamarr, actress, inventor (1913-2000)

Hedy Lamarr was creative, intelligent, and overcame a lot of obstacles in her life. She was willing to challenge the norms of society— in both lifestyle decisions that she made and in cinema. She left Europe because of the atrocities being committed by the Nazi regime. In America, Hedy Lamarr continued to associate with some of the most talented people in the Arts and Sciences. She had a successful Hollywood film career while passionately pursuing her own personal ideas. Her scientific work still influences the "technology boom" of the 21st century. Hedy Lamarr's long life was full of meaning, learning, and adventure.

◆

Albert Einstein, physicist (1879-1955)

Albert Einstein was the questioning student who tried to find his own way and meaning from life. He did not follow the "rules" if they threatened to hinder his research efforts. Einstein skipped classes that were not to his liking, he debated peers, and he looked for novel approaches to solving problems.

Einstein's ambition was to solve some of the mysteries of life. His unconventional thoughts would influence every scientist that followed him. Einstein had great dreams and goals, and even when most people doubted him, he firmly believed in himself.

Einstein struggled to obtain a job after his university education, because he had a lack of recommendations. His teachers disliked and/or were unable to appreciate his creative style of thinking. Einstein experienced financial difficulties and family problems, but he had the courage and determination to continue his quest to make scientific discoveries. And, when he made his discoveries, he was resilient in overcoming his detractors to make his voice heard by the world.

Josephine Baker, entertainer (1906-1975)

Josephine Baker overcame a lot of childhood crises to become a great artist and activist. When she realized that the United States was not ready to embrace her dancing, she journeyed to France to begin a scintillating career. She started fashion trends, and her unconventional approach to dancing and entertaining was lauded by the most celebrated artists and by the European public.

Josephine Baker was outspoken and powerful at a time when African-Americans were mistreated. She had a tremendous amount of pride and respect for herself. In the later stages of her life, Josephine Baker struggled through financial problems. But, these issues did not prevent her from increasing her creative output. She continued to give great performances until the end of her life.

Agnès Varda, film director (1928-present)

Agnès Varda is a pioneer in the film industry. She is one of the first great female directors. Varda's films cover controversial subjects; they range from the portrayal of a young woman finding more meaning in life during the time of her cancer diagnosis, to observing people who find a use for products which have been casted off by society. Her films are extraordinary, because they penetrate beyond the superficialities of life. People are not condemned for being unconventional. Instead, Agnès Varda gets us to better understand the unique perspectives of the people in her films— to empathize with their true feelings and thoughts, and to appreciate their determination to find meaning from both nature and their existence.

Edith Södergran, poet (1892-1923)

Edith Södergran was a Finnish poet. She endured poverty and sickness to become a preeminent Scandinavian writer. When she was young, her father died from tuberculosis. Sadly, she caught his disease, and this would ultimately lead to her early death. Her mother supported her for the short amount of time that she had left to live.

Although Södergran was frequently bedridden, she motivated herself to discover her reason for Being— and the essence of who she was as a person. Her poetry was influenced by both Nietzsche and by religion, but most of all by her exploration of her feelings while in solitude. Edith Södergran had a fondness for nature and a great sensitivity towards people. She believed that she could accomplish her dreams— that her willpower would allow her to overcome her misfortunes.

Södergran's poems reveal the spirit of a free-thinking individual who was searching for answers to life. Södergran had a great love for herself, and through her writings we get to know an authentic human being.

Marie Pleyel, pianist (1811-1875)

Marie Pleyel was one of the most outstanding pianists of the 19th century. Her music inspired the composers Berlioz and Liszt, as well as the great writer, Gèrard de Nerval. Pleyel overcame societal stereotypes of women of the day, and she became revered for her strength of character and for her humanity. She empathized for the suffering Nerval, and she befriended many people. Her success did not affect her creativity or her outlook on life. In later years, she married a great piano manufacturer of the day. Pleyel continued to perform with zeal, while having a great influence on her contemporaries in the Arts.

Max Ophüls, film director (1902-1957)

Max Ophüls is one of the most outstanding directors in the history of cinema. In the 1930s, he directed successful films in Germany and in other parts of Europe. The ravages resulting from Nazi atrocities forced him to re-start his career in the United States. He was able to persevere through the emotional pain of being separated from friends and the turmoil that was affecting his homeland. Max Ophüls did not let adversity detract from his vision for making films, and his movies were well-received in the United States.

In the last decade of his life, Max Ophüls returned to Western Europe to direct his artistic masterpieces. While financial success did not accompany these endeavors, his creative approach to filmmaking during these years has continued to influence directors.

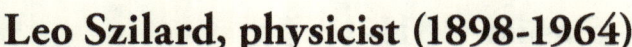

Leo Szilard, physicist (1898-1964)

Leo Szilard was a remarkable physicist and individual. He was continually thinking ahead of his time. When the Nazis invaded Europe, he departed at once. He believed that it was important to be intuitive and to act decisively. Szilard attributed this approach to saving his life in the 1930s.

Szilard was one of the brilliant minds behind the devising of the atomic bomb. Einstein had a tremendous amount of respect for him. They both feared that atomic energy could be misused— so Szilard, with Einstein's support, lobbied the world to be cautious with how it dealt with this vast source of energy.

Szilard always had hope— believing that he could prevail and overcome the odds. When Szilard was diagnosed with terminal cancer, he decided to create his own radiation treatment. Miraculously, Szilard cured himself for a short time. Leo Szilard was courageous in difficult times, and he continually tried to improve himself and the world.

Marc Chagall, painter (1887-1985)

Marc Chagall was born in Russia in the late 19th century. Since he was a Jew, there were many restrictions placed on his early life. Chagall was treated unfairly by artistic schools, because of his religious beliefs. Therefore, he left his family and roots behind, and traveled to Paris.

Marc Chagall was confident in his ability when he was poor and not recognized by the critics. Chagall experimented with his painting and he taught himself by observing the work of those around him— Picasso, Matisse, and the numerous other masters who were involved in the Modern art revolution. When World War I broke out, Chagall left Paris, and upon his return he was disappointed to find out that many of his paintings were missing. But, Chagall continued his work and challenged himself by undertaking monumental projects.

He faced more adversity with the onset of World War II and with the death of his beloved wife and muse, Bella. However, the difficult circumstances did not slow down Chagall. He began to work in a new medium— stained glass. He continued to paint throughout his long life.

Norman Lindsay, painter, writer (1879-1969)

Norman Lindsay was one of the most controversial and creative artists of the 20th century. The talented Australian excelled at painting, drawing, etching, and writing. Additionally, he successfully published books in the early 20th century.

Norman Lindsay came from a family of creative individuals who believed that it was important to express the true self. Norman Lindsay made sure that his life was consistent with his ideals. His outspoken views often attracted the ire of church and state officials. But, Lindsay would not compromise his beliefs for people who he saw as hypocritical and reactionaries.

Norman Lindsay was willing to stand up to people who he felt were trying to bully him to think in their narrow-minded way. Lindsay did not pretend to be flawless. And, there were times when he enjoyed shocking and provoking the public. Lindsay was a courageous innovator who thought a lot about life, nature, and the arts— and it were these qualities that enabled him to fulfill many of his dreams.

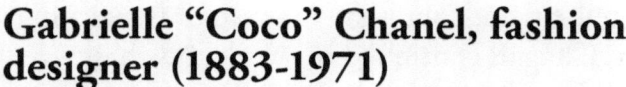

Gabrielle "Coco" Chanel, fashion designer (1883-1971)

Gabrielle "Coco" Chanel grew up poor. As a young adult, Chanel found the means to start her own fashion house, and she introduced an innovative style to dress designing. Her outfits would emphasize line and simplicity. She favored slacks and the suit for women. This was revolutionary, because it was previously expected that women would conform to long, flowing dresses and corsets.

Chanel also created the "little black dress," and devised her own perfume. Soon, celebrities and the "common person" were following the trends set by this woman with novel ideas. Chanel often defied the rules of society. At times, she dressed like a man, and she was not afraid to express her controversial views or enjoy life in her own way. She befriended Modern artists such as Lipschitz and Cocteau, and in turn, they supported her endeavors.

In middle age, Chanel temporarily left haute couture. During this time, World War II was taking place. In later years, she made a stunning comeback to the fashion scene. Many critics had doubted that she would be able to succeed. They felt that her approaches were outdated. However, the confident Chanel proved them wrong. She reinvigorated the industry, and continued to live on her own terms.

Christian Dior, fashion designer (1905-1957)

Christian Dior was sensitive to beauty from an early age. During his youth, he admired the flowers that surrounded his French country home. At the beginning of his career, Dior was an assistant to a well-known fashion designer. He was shy, and initially he was pleased to use his creative talents in a role that would not put him in direct contact with clientele or with the fashion writers. However, when the opportunity came to run his own fashion house, Dior seized the opportunity.

Christian Dior remained kind and gentle to his friends and associates. But, Dior was a strong, determined, and innovative man too. He made creative decisions, while being willing to consider the thoughts and feelings of his assistants. It was only a short time before his fashions were highly sought after throughout the world. Dior's inspiration came from within— he revisited the dreams of his childhood and explored his inner-self. Christian Dior worked at what he loved— and this brought him fulfillment in life.

Sidonie-Gabrielle Colette, writer (1873-1954)

Colette used her life experiences as inspiration for her writings. She was a rebel— and often ready to flout norms of the day. Colette persevered through the stressful times of her first marriage. She was mistreated by this husband, and he took credit for her work. Once she decided to sever the relationship, Colette began to experience fulfillment in her life. Her writings were embraced throughout the world. And, her intimate writing style influenced diarists and authors.

Colette had friendships with many of the artists of her era. As she grew older, health problems became a concern. She had to make changes in her lifestyle. But, this would not prevent her from creatively expressing her thoughts and feelings. Colette continued to make her voice heard through her writings.

Marie Laurencin, artist (1883-1956)

Marie Laurencin developed as an artist by experimenting and learning from and with her friends— which included Picasso and Apollinaire. While the Cubists were in vogue, Laurencin went her own, feminine way. She found success and meaning in her life by painting delicate portraits of women and flowers. World War I forced her into exile, away from her friends. However, she continued her great creative output when she returned. She designed some sets for Diaghilev, along with continuing to paint and illustrate novels from renowned writers. Marie Laurencin did not want to be like her contemporaries. She was insistent on following her own ideals and dreams.

Publicity still photo of Greta Garbo

Words of Wisdom and Letters from Inspiring Personalities of the Past

Cataclysms, bombs, and upheavals. If you have a seismograph in your heart, then it is your duty to sense when I have an agitated week.
– Pierre Louÿs, early 20th century fiction writer and poet

Increase Creativity by → expressing your feelings

My new publisher Alan Swallow is wonderful and will have all the books out by Fall, including long out of print Winter of Artifice. This has been my year. I was interested in your remarks on Larry. It is true I have concentrated on the women— but I felt we all knew less about women. However, I will try to tell more about men. I do in fact know them.
– Anaïs Nin, celebrated diarist and writer

Increase Creativity by → being receptive to change and continually learning about yourself

Dear Charlie-

Grace and I cannot tell you how sorry we (regal we, that is) were that you couldn't make it over for the ceremony— it was very quiet, just the family and no publicity— see you soon, Best always—"Rainy"

P.S. The large knife (ceremonial sword) I have hanging on left side, is the one I killed M the 3 eyed lion with.

Uncle Charlie,

Rainy is so naughty. Marriage has not changed me! I still love my dear Uncle Charlie. Princess Grace.

- Prince Rainier and Princess Grace de Monaco, Royalty, legendary film actress

Increase Creativity by ➜ having fun, being witty, and having a youthful spirit

Dear Friend,

You came— I was in my bath— I went downstairs— You had disappeared! I don't understand it all- Did you come by car? Come whenever you want to share bread and cheese— That's all that's left!!!

- Isadora Duncan, pioneer and founder of Modern Dance

Increase Creativity by → sharing with others and forming caring relationships

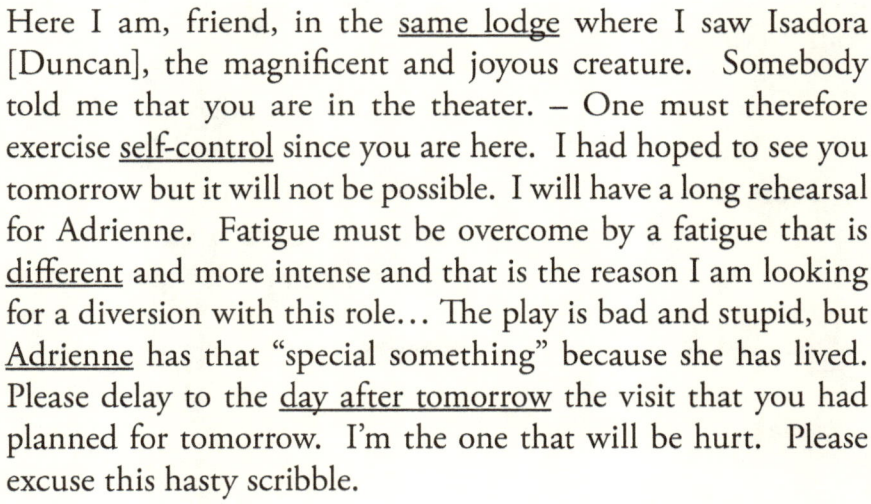

Here I am, friend, in the <u>same lodge</u> where I saw Isadora [Duncan], the magnificent and joyous creature. Somebody told me that you are in the theater. – One must therefore exercise <u>self-control</u> since you are here. I had hoped to see you tomorrow but it will not be possible. I will have a long rehearsal for Adrienne. Fatigue must be overcome by a fatigue that is <u>different</u> and more intense and that is the reason I am looking for a diversion with this role... The play is bad and stupid, but <u>Adrienne</u> has that "special something" because she has lived. Please delay to the <u>day after tomorrow</u> the visit that you had planned for tomorrow. I'm the one that will be hurt. Please excuse this hasty scribble.

- Eleanora Duse, great 19th-20th century stage actress

Increase Creativity by → being inspired by creative personalities, becoming immersed in the Arts, and observing the positives of experiences in life

I am sending you a very dear friend who leaves tomorrow for London. I think you would like to have my news. I think very often about you. With much affection and many memories of your kindness to me,

- Isadora Duncan, pioneer and founder of Modern Dance

Increase Creativity by ➙ **helping other people and continuing to nurture special relationships**

I was unable to meet with you yesterday and today I cannot go out. So I am writing you because I need your advice – here it is. Do you have a rich friend who is interested in helping artists? Or a capitalist who is looking for a deal? I find myself in rather difficult circumstances and am in immediate need of thirty thousand francs to remedy the situation and give me the peace of mind essential for my artistic pursuits. Thanks to your suggestions and support, I have enjoyed a successful career that I want to pursue and enhance through the creation of ballets… As collateral for this loan that I will pay back in two or three years, I offer my performances less the money that is owed you and everything in my town house including the horses and the carriages. I put my faith in you, dear Mr. Astruc. I am a stranger here and it is only to you that I can express these thoughts.

– Mata Hari, early 20th century dancer, alleged spy

Increase Creativity by ➔ **persevering and overcoming obstacles, listening to the thoughts and feelings of others, making your creative talents known to others, willing to ask trustworthy people for help— you cannot do everything by yourself, and being assertive**

I am forming a syndicate now nearly complete of American papers to receive a weekly London by me of bright and varied gossip. Should you be willing to join no other paper in your town would be supplied. The subscription is $ 2.50 and the length one column. An early answer will oblige.

Yours truly, Loie Fuller

   – Loie Fuller, 1889 letter, pioneer Modern dancer

Increase Creativity by → **embarking on new endeavors, looking forward to challenges, making others interested in your creative product or service, and having an optimistic outlook**

Dear Lili,

The times during the past 20 years were such that one rarely had the ease to send friends signs of life, or even signs of survival. Also, I scarcely knew whether the friends were still alive. Well— your dear postcard, which reached me here two days ago, bridges all this anxious uncertainty, and I thank you for having taken the initiative in contacting me. Who knows what may still become of the Schwarzenbergplatz. It is nice to know that throughout all of these changes, you have kept faith with me, and it is self-understood that I will visit you when I come to Vienna. Of course I have not forgotten how you took care of me in those days, how you stood by me, and I have often spoken about you with Hansel when I met him in emigration, and also often with Hilde, who still is my "Schwarzenbergplatz." I am certain that she sends you many greetings, and she has promised to write to you within the next days. We wish you all the best. Do let us know particulars and also tell me how you liked my film, but honestly. If you find fault with it, then say so.

Cordially yours,

Max

My dear Lili,

I am always happy when you occasionally think of me so dearly and faithfully. Unfortunately, I still cannot arrange to come to Vienna. Hilde also sends her greetings. We not only wish you that your finger improves soon, but that you are well in general. We have never forgotten the good that you did us when we were young and depended on any kind of moral help.

I also still remember your picture. Are there no photographs of it? If so, please do send one. I will then show it to our Lola

Montes, who must go to a lot of trouble to be as beautiful as you were.

> Sincere greetings,
> Yours,
> Max

–   Max Ophüls, film director, 1951 and 1955 letters

Increase Creativity by → **o v e r c o m i n g a d v e r s i t y, helping others, continuing to be creative— even when experiencing hardships, being receptive to constructive criticism, and continually being supportive of special people in your life**

Search amongst seven great women of our times, between the Empress of China and Matilde Serao, between Madame Sada Yacco and Madame Curie, the history of Madame F. and the truth of these people. Search well. Reflect on the reason for this and I wait for this history. I am not a little surprised that this is not known.

– Pierre Louÿs, early 20th century fiction writer and poet

Increase Creativity by → being self-reflective, analyzing your knowledge and extending it to form new thoughts, and pursuing new experiences in your life

---

Dear Sir,

Thank you for your kind letter. I am sending you my book "Prufrock." With regard to the most characteristic work, I am not able to find any particular poem. "Prufrock" is the one which attracted the most attention. But, look in your own way, the lines are not numerous, it is not too artful! Please send me a copy of your study, and be sure, Sir, of my deep sympathy.

T.S. Eliot

– T.S. Eliot, poet, 1920 letter

Increase Creativity by → forming your own, unique feelings and thoughts and willing to be unconventional

---

Well, here I am, but you do not have the right to reprove me because it's not my fault, which means that instead of the declaration of war that you threatened, I expect to hear a few statements of friendship and consolation from you. You won't deny me that, I hope.

I have another request of you, you see, like a real country fellow I come to you with my pockets full of solicitations and petitions, etc. etc. Would you be so kind as to ask Mr. Fournier to return a written note that I signed for him here at the beginning of August when he came to make a proposal for his theater? Since his plans are dead and buried, that paper can't be of the least bit of importance to him, but it would mean a lot to me to have it back. By the way, in my experience Mr. Fournier has always been so friendly and obliging that I am convinced he won't try to cross me by refusing. I should point out to you that I have already written to him on the matter without getting a response, but I attribute that to his preoccupation with his post as director which doesn't leave him enough time on his hands.

Sorry about this long letter of such meager consequence. I would only be asking an enemy like you for such a service, and I count on all your sincere friendship of which you have already given me so much proof.

Think well of me and know that I will always be your devoted.

M. Pleyel.

   – Marie Pleyel, celebrated 19th century female pianist

Increase Creativity by ➔ **having a "playful" spirit, expressing your sincere feelings and thoughts to people who care about**

**you, trying to understand
how others feel, being
resilient, and recognizing
that overcoming mistakes
can inspire originality and
strengthen relationships**

———————— ◆ ◆ ◆ ————————

Who is who with the look blasé
Who is who that acts passé
Who is who that is la belle…
It is Gussa
A stuck up elegant mollusk
Like a mussel with Stiller as its husk
She has been plastered on Berlin's billboards
And been quoted in every newspaper word by word
Filmjornalen has her in their care
In Scandal she has Swedish record
Erotiken is one of her…

 – Greta Garbo, actress, poem that she wrote about herself
 and Mauritz Stiller

**Increase Creativity by → learning more about your
thoughts and feelings
from writing and reading,
realizing that we all have
imperfections— but that
your flaws can help you
to discover unique and
meaningful paths in life**

———————— ◆ ◆ ◆ ————————

Please forgive me for taking so long to thank you for your dear letters— I can't tell you how much I appreciated hearing from you both and your words of sympathy and understanding have touched me deeply. One is so grateful for loving friends at these times.

- Princess Grace de Monaco (Grace Kelly), princess, actress, letter to Brian Aherne

Increase Creativity by → appreciating the love and support from people who mean a lot to you, and always having faith in yourself— it is your love for and belief in yourself that enables you to overcome challenges

ABOUT THE AUTHOR

Blake Bazel, M.S. Clinical Psychology, is a Creativity researcher and editor of the book *Creativity Defined*. Also, his writing has been featured in the Association for Humanistic Psychology's *Perspective* magazine.

www.ingramcontent.com/pod-product-compliance
Lightning Source LLC
Chambersburg PA
CBHW021230280526
45784CB00005B/2040